*Heaven's
Headache*
*

Heaven's Headache

*An in-depth look into the Book of Jonah and
the message the prophet has for us today*

....

By R. D. Knighten

HEAVEN'S HEADACHE | An in-depth look into the Book of Jonah and the message the prophet has for us today

ISBN 978-0-9911412-1-0

Printed in the United States of America

Scriptures taken from the New King James Version ®

To the lost souls of this generation:

The depressed, the disadvantaged, and those contemplating suicide;
Those who are unfulfilled and held down by their addictions,
The hurt, confused, and each one of you sinking in seas of despair-

I dedicate this book.

Table of Contents

Preface

We all have been given a vision. It is the very thing that drives us. As young men and women we expected our futures to be wonderful and full of adventure. Even in adulthood we commit to personal goals because we seek constant improvement. For early preparation, parents have visions for their children. At times parents set high expectations for their child's future before the child can walk.

Having a vision usually means we have a clear standard upon which our vision can exist. We don't have dreams that are impossible to achieve or else we'd quickly forget them. The vision must be attainable and it must be realistic.

To have a vision also means we have confidence in our resolve to see it through. Each of us have experienced the feeling of accomplishment because at some point of our lives we stayed the course. The reward often outweighs the struggle. Inside our mind the seed was planted and through our work we toiled until we saw visible results.

As believers we walk in the vision that God has for this world. He has expectations and standards we are commanded to follow. The challenge comes in the case that God doesn't literally speak to each individual person. Instead, God speaks through us by providing us with physical abilities, the mental aptitude, and spiritual convictions for the purpose of expressing to us His intentions.

Because of our carnality, many people refuse to tap into their gift. It is certifiably inaccurate to assume that all ignorance is bliss. As a consequence of worldly influence, many people will rather subscribe to a vision that a fraudulent social order provides for them. I have known for a very long time what God's purpose for my life would be. It took some time before I actually allowed my gift to manifest beyond my "mental-scape". Thankfully I allowed myself the opportunity to develop my ability because God would later allow me to see His vision through my gift.

Creating this book would be the first opportunity to get God's intentions on paper. I was afraid to do so because there is nothing, in my opinion, that qualifies me to have this literary conversation, or speak to the concept of this book. Immediately I began to point out why I wasn't competent enough to write the book. It's obvious that I'm no million dollar televangelist. I'm not a popular theologian or leader of a mega-church who graces the stage of sold out arenas and venues across the nation.

I feared the first thing many readers would do is search for my credentials. What merits have compelled this guy to write this book?

Secondly, I feared others would look into my physical appearance to see if I match up to the depth of this dialogue. Apparently there's a certainly look one must have to be a credible source of spiritual retort. In my doubtful mind I had given a face to God's message and to the messenger.

I had to move pass my own cynicism. Nothing can exclude us from the potential that God has given us - His creation.

Consider this: What makes a poor kid from Indiana dream of becoming great? Simple! He knew the potential locked inside of him and this helped to steer his destiny. His vision was far greater than his family's economic situation, the lack of book smarts, and the negativity he faced daily. His mother wasn't always available since she worked two jobs to support the boy and his four siblings. His father had given up on life and committed suicide before the young man even finished high school. This kid had every reason to define himself by his situation. He could have allowed his living conditions and the absence of viable resources to cloud his decision making. Nevertheless, he "powered forward" and is now considered as one of the greatest NBA stars to have ever played the game of basketball.

Larry Bird was not birthed to fit inside the proverbial box that society suggests he, or any of us, should be in due to our economic state. Our imperfections do not define us. If someone actually based the merits of this book according to anything beyond my potential, they would miss out on a thoughtful, well-examined read. With this in mind, I pressed on.

Sadly, in today's world, people are committed to a life of artificial nuances. They subject themselves to a distorted view of the world and govern their lives according to it. For centuries, these devices have been used to shape people's thoughts, emotions, and entire personalities.

There are very few people that exist freely in this world. Media and social trends have threatened our ability to think at an elevated level – or decide for ourselves. Over time these devices have invaded our neural passages and have gradually stripped us of our individuality. It has glazed our views and tinted our perceptions.

Before we proceed, please understand that this world is made of a variety of components both visible and invisible. We all perceive the mechanics of this life based on the truths upon which our experiences are built. Therefore, what is real to you may not be real to another. In this respect, the things you have come to appreciate may not be adequately recognized or widely accepted as a priority for someone else.

It's no coincidence that among all of the experiences we do have in common resides the many mysteries of Heaven – Earth's counterpart.

At whatever level, both believers and non-believers attribute feelings of love and compassion to a sensory beyond human capacity. The faithful life is not an easy one but we've all had an encounter, in spirit or flesh, with our Creator.

We can find scientific ways to explain it and develop technologies to examine it. The fact remains that the spirit of God moves through each of us which provides a wormhole for God's plan to be manifested here on Earth. Humans are simply a collection of bridges in a universal portal connecting Heaven to Earth. (Matthew 6:10)

With this being said, understand that each individual has a purpose. You play a major role in the building of the Kingdom of God, which is administered through His Son, Jesus the Christ.

The Book Of Jonah

In order to tell a story we must first identify the setting. It's also important to know how the characters interact within these various locations and landmarks. Here's a very brief history of each city mentioned in *The Book of Jonah*.

Gath-hepher

Very little is known of the town of Gath-hepher. The Bible says that the prophet's family were native to the village. Gath-hepher lies west of the Sea of Galilee. Over time the city underwent many periods of change, just as the rest of the nation of Israel had. The splitting of the nation, various wars and occupations, and religious influences caused the dynamics of the entire land to evolve. The town of Gath-hepher occupied an area which would later fold into the urban complex known as Nazareth. Some sources depict ancient Nazareth being renowned for its architectural beauty and skillful mastery in masonry. Other sources say the isolated city was a small village which agriculture was the primary occupation. Centuries later, Nazareth would become the center where a young couple from Bethlehem would relocate to raise their children.

Joseph and Mary's son, Jesus (Yeshua) spent his childhood and adolescent years in the city. Understanding the social dynamic of the town, it's not surprising that Jesus's trade interest was in carpentry. His profession is mentioned in Mark 6:3 and Mathew 13:55.

Nazarene life inspired Jesus as he was exposed to great minds and affluent civic leaders, but mostly the young man witnessed terrible bigotry and poverty.

Joppa

Joppa (jah'puh), modern day Tel-Aviv, was situated on the

Mediterranean coast and its name means "beautiful" in Hebrew. Joppa (Yaffo) was located some thirty-five miles northwest of Jerusalem. Excavations have revealed that the city dates back at least to 1650 B.C. It is one of the oldest port cities on the Mediterranean coastline.

Joppa may also be a variation of the Greek "Jafe" who is the daughter of the god Aeolus, god of the winds. The Second Chronicles lists Joppa as the port where King Solomon imported wood from Lebanon that was used to build the first temple in Jerusalem. A considerable amount of his lavish exports were hauled in through the coastal hub.

After the Pentecost recorded in the nineth chapter of The Book of Acts, it's possible that a group of enthusiastic North African missionaries, returning to their homelands, evangelized in Joppa and set up a Christian colony there. Sometime later, the Disciple Peter would find there was a fervently established sect there; although he was oddly invited to the city to attend a funeral. After the miraculous resurrection of Saint Tabitha, Peter works encouraged the colony during his journey there.

Tarshish

It is widely accepted among ministers and scholars that the prophet's eyes were set to the southern coast town Tartessos in Spain. The actual whereabouts of the city has broadly been the subject of debate more so than *The Book of Jonah* in its entirety.

The Prophet Daniel names the Mediterranean as the "sea of Tarshish." This definitely rules out Tartessos, since the sea in proximity to Tartessos is the Atlantic Ocean. Look at the word Tarshish and consider the Arabic dialect as heard in the stressing of the "sh" digraph. By simply removing the "h" from the word Tarshish we arrive at "Tarsis", or Tarsus. This notion adds to the debate of places where Jonah may have been heading toward. This book supports the later argument.

Tarsus is located on the southern border of Cilicia, modern day Turkey, and has been an important commercial port since 2300 B.C. Jonah may have desired to retreat from the monotonous, slow paced hillside of east Galilee he was used to. Just as he had heard of the atrocities taking place in Nineveh, he had most likely heard of the decadent culture of Tarshish. Jonah set his sights seaward and embarked on a cruise traveling due north.

Tarsus was esteemed for its cultural and economic influence. The Bible speaks of the abundance of precious metals and rare minerals found in of the province which also boasts to its affluence. Saul, a native of Tarsus, who later became known as the Apostle Paul, is transformed miraculously on his route through Damascus.

Nineveh

Nineveh was revered as the war-ridden capital of the Assyrian Empire, a formidable threat across the Eastern world. The Assyrians were known to be ruthless in war and fierce in combat. It is said that in celebration of their victories, citizens would decorate the city walls with the skins of their enemies. They also impaled men, women, and children, and placed their bodies on poles and lit them afire as street lamps. It seems this barbarism, much of which occurred after they discharged from the battlefields, was intended to create a legacy of violence. This tactic unquestionably struck fear into their neighboring adversaries. This growing reputation of demonic brutality would prove to be one of their greatest weapons.

Assyria not only had a culture of war but the nation also produced great artists, thinkers, and even greater monarchs.

King Hammurabi (c. 1792-c. 1750 BC) is one of the most impressive historical figures of the ancient Middle Eastern world. His legislative precepts have preceded him via his Code of

Hammurabi. The codes were a system of law which was carved in marble, discovered in the 20th century and published in 1911. The book of law gives 280 judgments on civil and criminal law. In addition to governmental affairs, the Code of Hammurabi the king lists all nations and roughly 24 cities that were amassed under his emperorship. Nineveh was his most prized possession.

Astarte, also called Ashtoreth, was worshipped by the Assyrians during the reign of King Solomon. She was known as the Queen of Heaven by the Canaanites and praised for her qualities of sexual love and war tactics. King Solomon commissioned the building of the temple to honor his wives who were former residents of the foreign country. In his book "History of the Cross", published in 1871, author Henry Dana Ward mentions the widespread acceptance of the idol in ancient civilization:

"Her character was established from Egypt to India, and she is represented as found on the monuments of Egypt, on the coins and medals of Syria, and on the ruins dug out of Nineveh, holding in her hand a long scepter, of the form of the Roman augur's wand, which is the same with the bishop's staff or crozier, wearing the crescent on her head." (Ward, pg. 18)

Astarte was the counterpart to the goddess Ishtar. Nineveh was said to be protected by the female deity. Ishtar was the Mesopotamian goddess of fertility and war. Some idolized variations are found depicting the pagan goddess as an owl, a bull, and ironically as a fish. She is the daughter of Sin (or Anu), the Sumerian god of the Moon. This provides an even stronger backdrop to Jonah's mission, and furthermore substantiates the scriptural evidence of his descend into the belly of the whale.

The purpose of this explanation is to prove that the

Ninevites were *"gods*-fearing" people. Incidentally, they were piously idolatrous. For centuries they had been groomed in transcendent devotion. This presented a great opportunity for God to monopolize on their divine ambitions and redirect this predisposition of intense submission to divination. Though they had many deities, God sought to capitalize on the many vacancies (love, salvation, etc) that those deities had abandoned.

Jonah Ben Ammatai

Very few scholars have made mention of how the story of the prophet, Jonah Ben Ammatai, segments that of the prophet Jesus of Nazareth. The following is a brief background description of our protagonist.

The Prophet Jonah, or "Yunus" in Arabic, was believed to prophesy in Israel in the later part of the 700th century. His name is often translated as "dove" in Hebrew. Doves are regarded as a symbol of peace. Some have translated his name as meaning "bringer of peace". Ironically, during his episode in defiance towards God, whatever paths he treaded so followed suffering and discontent. Nonetheless you will discover later that he would usher in peace for an entire community of people. Unfortunately, he would be reluctant to indulge in it himself.

The Prophet Jonah is mentioned very few times in the Holy text but has notoriety above most of the Minor Prophets. He is regarded as a champion of the faith and as a premier specimen of spiritual fortitude. However, in the telling of his own story Jonah is sadly observed as a prideful, thoughtless slacker.

Oddly enough, his father's name means "truth." Not much is known about Ammatai. He is not mentioned in any other biblical books or historical writings. We can only assume that he was a stand-up guy who raised his son in the way of the Lord. Jonah's solid upbringing could have certainly prepared him for a life of service leading up to being given the designation of the prophet of Israel.

Taking Action

The sign of the prophet Jonah not only serves as a sign of things to come. Within the sign is the evidence of Christ's death and resurrection. Being raised on the third morning following his burial, Jesus fulfilled God's vision to hold his people under a new standard – grace through faith. Christ's resurrection signified that mankind would no longer be subjected to the many tenets of Abrahamic Law due to the establishment of the faith. Through faith all things are possible and Jesus lived faith to the extreme. Being an example of immeasurable faith, he held others accountable to experience the benefits as well.

The parallel between Jesus and Jonah are similar in that for three days both had descended into a dark abyss. During these days the two were completely separated from God. Although Jesus' sentence was purposefully executed, Jonah's was not. Jonah's had fallen as result of his own irrationality. As a prophet he was committed to a life of obedience and purity. So, why would a man with so much favor, shy away from his destiny when he had committed his life to such an obligation? This answer is simple. Jonah was a man.

1 JOHN 4:18
FEAR GOING FORTH

"There is no fear in love; but perfect love casts out fear, because fear involves torment. But he who fears has not been made perfect in love."

Prophet Jonah, in his weakness, allowed fear and doubt to compromise his confidence in God's plan. We all have been guilty of it. Within the doctrinal premises in defining our lives, we discover this innate human flaw. This flaw is sealed around an idea that is pivotal to the radical ministry of Jesus Christ.

When we examine the entire dialogue that is had in Matthew 16th chapter between Jesus and the Pharisees, we see that they were the common archetype of many folks today. They challenge the merits of holiness and only accept the things which can be proven scientifically.

Jesus understood this sort of behavior. It did not make him happy to witness his words falling on death ears. Regardless of the sound advice and wisdom he offered, there would be a significant portion of his impromptu congregations that would merely shrug their shoulders to his message of delivery and salvation.

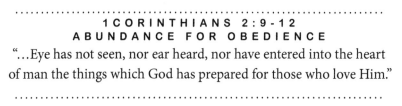

1 CORINTHIANS 2:9-12
ABUNDANCE FOR OBEDIENCE
"...Eye has not seen, nor ear heard, nor have entered into the heart of man the things which God has prepared for those who love Him."

From his suspicious heart the Pharisee spoke and asked the guest teacher if he'd offer a sign. The scribe had requested an indicator so that he could know when the prophecy was to be fulfilled. They wanted to know, in retrospect, how long they had before they'd be held accountable for their actions, decisions, and deeds. These men saw no need to engage in their beliefs publically as an example for their people to follow. They did not want to work nor change their lifestyles or habits.

Falling In Line

Mediocrity is at an all-time high. We tend to prefer things written out plainly. As of late, everyone seems to be too busy doing nothing. Many of us have no time to spare for personal achievement or development. Even members of the faith community fall into this territory. Christians often give The Father pennies and expect him to make dollars from them.

Jesus was not a magician either. He came to fulfill the scriptures which promised the Hebrews a present redeemer. He was not a manipulator of signs and symbols. The only thing that he could offer is the truth; therefore he revealed to them their true nature.

He told the local bureaucracy that there would be no sign. These men of sociopolitical influence failed to grasp the concept of soul-searching and self-realization. Just as much of his ministry was recorded through parables, Jesus Christ had indirectly challenged them with truth. To the fail of their own misinterpretation of the Law, the men had fashioned their entire lives around their individual understanding of the content within the Old Testament. The problem is that they had gotten comfortable seeing the promise of deliverance inked on papyrus and were unwilling to recognize it within their hearts.

According to Jesus, the sign, in retrospect, would not be something immediately distinguishable. It would not be something we could gage by celestial events or by bleeps on a radar detector. Instead, it is within us, fixated to our consciousness and it is up to us to either accept it or deny it. He said, "I am the way, the truth, and the light," to illustrate how he would be the human prototype for us to follow.

The biopic recorded of Jonah in many ways resembles one that we too shall write. He was a common man assigned to complete an unpopular task. He accepted his initial calling but would later find himself trekking rearward away from an important course of action.

Bound By Fear

I'm sure that we'd run out of fingers counting the many times we start our day with a goal then fail to follow through. There are many of us who have made commitments with our talents and gifts but unexpectedly we lose interest, quit, or procrastinate in our pursuits.

So why don't we make more of an effort to seize the opportunity to develop our ideas? One reason is due to all the external distractions around. Many of us find ourselves allowing the outside world to hinder us from our internal instinct to be productive.

It's not uncommon to question our inability to jumpstart our dreams or even getting frustrated in the pursuit of them. In most cases it's the fear of failure that hinders our progress. As a rule, we should begin to ask ourselves "why are we doing this?" before we can make an attempt to see our ideas come alive. Simon Sinek states in his book, *Start With Why,* that fear is a powerful manipulator:

"When fear is employed, facts are incidental. Deeply seated in our biological drive to survive, that emotion cannot be quickly wiped away with facts and figures. This is how terrorism works. It's not the statistical probability that one could get hurt by a terrorist, but it's the fear that it might happen that cripple a population."

We'd have more of a chance at success if we were to push ahead rather than quit.

2 TIMOTHY 1:7
DEFINING FEAR
"For God has not given us a spirit of fear, but of power and of love and of a sound mind."

Fear is a wall that we create. It doesn't exist in the real world yet it manifests itself through our emotions, actions, and principles in specific real-world matters. Much of our society therefore is configured on the illusion of fear. Fear is often translated and sold in the form of security. Many businesses have exploited fear as a tactic to create demand. Advanced security devices monitor our homes, vehicles, and offices. Various insurances are sold to protect our financial livelihood in the event of a sudden death or other unforseen events. Fear is also a major contributor to the rise and fall of stock prices. In this arena fear controls the stockholder towards the buying or selling of a "security." The way he/she perceives the graphical data, media coverage, and information provided for the security directly influences trade behavior.

As a guide for living, Mr. Sinek advises that one should frequently employ aspiration to fend off any emotional doubt. If we find ourselves in the realm of doubt and uncertainty, we should look at the people and things that inspire us. Also, when in distress, we should begin to consider the original purpose for our ambitious stabs at success. Most of us immediately name our family as the reasons for our daily fuel of determination. Others will claim money – lots of it.

At the core of our desire to succeed lies subtleties that make up the foundations of success; the things that we are humanly entitled to. Comfort, peace, respect, pride, etc. are things that money can't buy. These are the very items that the government, the media, and culture have either perverted or repackaged for us, which in turn has skewed the true meaning of success.

If you've thought long and hard about your *whys*, write them down. If you haven't already, be sure to include the word "freedom" on your list. This is the foundation where your *why* can firmly stand.

You owe it to yourself to obtain comfort, peace, and all the things that would offer you lasting memories. However, more than any of these things, you deserve freedom.

Freedom trumps all other emotions. It's a substance that the basic human emotions, like happiness, can be subcategorized under. To have comfort you must have the freedom to attain things that promote a comfortable lifestyle. To have the ability to go on random vacations and spend quality time with your kids, you will first need the freedom of availability and possibly even financial freedom. The list goes on.

At the signing of The Declaration of Independence in 1776, the men of the Second Continental Congress were all in agreement that all men should exist freely. Each person on this Earth must be given a chance to create a solid life for himself. They should not be bound to a template or format to fit into a particular standard. Fast forwarding three-hundred years to the present, when we consider our freedom to be, it instantly provokes a sense of pure independance. By humanity's rule, we all have these unalienable rights that should not be violated by any law, institute, or structure. We are who we are and should be allowed to express ourselves by any means that honors our individuality. This is what inspires imagination and ingenuity.

As a reflection of our Creator we must always remember foremost to exhibit integrity. We have a responsibility to our Creator to function within the environments that He has designated for us. The gifts we have been granted are for His glory alone and not for our own self-interests.

The following chapters will take an in-depth glance into the life of Jonah. By delving in and thoroughly examining the scripture, we will uncover the intrinsic value that the four chapters of his life offer to today's believer. Moving forward, these words will uncover the role that confidence, faith, and grace plays in our personal growth and spiritual development.

The Prophet Defined

Matthew 12:39
39 But He answered and said to them, "An evil and adulterous generation seeks after a sign, and no sign will be given to it except the sign of the prophet Jonah.

THE PROPHET DEFINED

Although he lived thousands of years ago, the spirit of the
Prophet Jonah still exists today. *The Book of Jonah* is not so
much about his ministry as much as it is prophetic to the lives we
experience today. Interestingly enough, many of the emotions he
had, and conclusions he came to, are ones we all can relate to.

This era in antiquity was not as simple as some would imagine.
War, death, and sickness were commonplace in the centuries
recorded in the Bible. Today's world is similar in that manner, but
now we have modernized concerns. Cyber terrorism, identity theft,
nuclear threats, and biological warfare are just a few additional
threats that interrupt our freedom to seek fulfilling lives.

The fact that we have become slaves to these fears has also
hindered our disposition to be openhearted. This world has
sadly influenced us into becoming unproductive, unfaithful, and
inconsiderate people. Jonah's brief story mirrors the flaw in our
modern civilization. *The Book of Jonah* ministers to us in hopes
to expose our own vulnerabilities. It's a fact that the four chapters
only account for a short portion of his ministry. Nevertheless each
section offers a very significant depiction of our individual reaction
to these troubling conditions.

An in-depth examination of his story forces us to face the
things that prevent us from moving forward in life. Jonah's
tale proves a pattern we all have, at some point, fallen into. We
stumble, pick ourselves up, and stumble again with each time
being worse than the last.

His story has not been deconstructed in this manner. For
spiritual leaders, there doesn't seem to be much to preach on
because very little is offered. Following the typical evaluation
of the book, we make the mistake of summing up Jonah's entire
plight to one passage – the big fish's brunch.

We do an injustice to his legacy by doing so. The Prophet
offers much more value than the faith community has openly

acknowledged.

It's a known fact that Jonah was a prophet for Israel. A prophet is defined as a leader claiming divine inspiration to proclaim the will of God. Usually when we think of a prophet we think of a psychic. Jonah could not see into the future. As a matter of fact, most Abrahamic faiths shun against wizardry, fortune-telling, and the making of arbitrary predictions. The future is not for us to predict. Therefore Jonah could not forsee exactly what he was getting himself into.

Prophet Jonah was given a message by God and his responsibility was to carry this message to those who needed to hear it. His purpose was different than his gift. His gift was his ability to hear God's holy command. However, Jonah's purpose, or the reason he was born, was to be a vessel for God's holy command to prevail in the physical realm.

Though his biography is short and leaves out a plethora of information regarding his extended ministry, we are not without a glimpse of the significant role he's played in establishing God's Kingdom here on Earth. It's critical to God that these gifts flow through us spiritually. Realize above all, that our purpose will always materialize itself through our physical actions.

Maybe not at the distinction of Jonah, but in a way we are all prophets. God can do nothing on Earth without man. We all exist to fulfill a particular duty commissioned by the spiritual realm so it's important that the spirit and the flesh compliment each other.

The goal of the believer is to do the will of God and to be a blessing to those coming into, and lost outside of, the fold of the Word of God. It is a valiant cause and one that is essential as we continue throughout this critical life endeavor. We are called to confront all things through faith. It is the power of faith that wills us in our pursuits to please God.

PSALMS 37:9
DIVINE PRIVILEGE
"For evildoers shall be cut off; But those who wait on the Lord,
They shall inherit the earth."

· ·

It was once explained to me that horses make "horses, dogs make dogs, cats make cats, but God makes gods." By no means does this insinuate that we are equal beings to the nature of our Creator. Rather, it is a discourse to our capacity at the physical level (lower spiritual frequency) to produce and nurture both animate and inanimate entities within the framework of our human capabilities. It also speaks to the presence of a physical and cognitive joint connection that we all individually share as an extension of the Creator. Simply put, we are more than a reflection of his work. Mankind is the earthly manifestation of His autonomous sovereignty in the universe.

We as believers are the beneficiaries of the promises to come. We set the stage for the Kingdom of Heaven to be established here on Earth. It's our goal to encourage and hold one another accountable. The faith community's duty is to help others redefine success in this age. It is no longer money or the accumulation of material items that identify God's people as "successful." Instead it's the understanding of the role you play as His chosen instrument. Success is how you utilize your gifts and the manner which you exert your potential here on Earth. By committing your life to the Lord and the utilization of these gifts, you will discover peace and experience wealth beyond the physical dimension.

It is my prayer that you will receive this publication as a sufficient guide in your life because it is produced and directed by the will of God. As a fellow believer, I am certain that through Jesus Christ you will have everything that you need to move forward in life. The Canadian-born actor and evangelical Art Linkletter said, "Everything happens for the best for those who make the best of what happens."

No longer shall depression, anxiety, fear, anguish, or unnecessary hurt exist in your life. God has planted a seed of purpose and potential within us all. The sooner we fully understand this, the better opportunity we have to give God our best.

The Doubting Man

Jonah 1:1-3

1 Now the word of the Lord came to Jonah the son of Ammatai, saying,

2 "Arise, go to Nineveh, that great city, and cry out against it; for their wickedness has come up before Me."

3 But Jonah arose to flee to Tarshish from the presence of the Lord. He went down to Joppa, and found a ship going to Tarshish; so he paid the fare, and went down into it, to go with them to Tarshish from the presence of the Lord.

When Jonah received his orders from God, he began to pack items into his travel bag. The trip to Nineveh was a mere three day trip; though it was most likely tough for a single guy going at it alone. Then again, it may have also been a simple excursion for an unaccompanied traveler at that time. Jonah had no wife or kids hitched in-tow behind him.

I can image him searching around his home for necessary items and mentally logging all the essentials. Dried meats, plenty of water, two or three wardrobe changes, and a good book would ensure a quick and comfortable turnaround trip. He thought over the things that he might say to the Ninevite people. It would not be a simple task to influence the people to change, therefore his words would have to be precise, profound, and, all obvious factors involved, significant to their needs.

The night before, Jonah reflected over his agenda: Go to Nineveh, preach, come home, and get back to work. Indeed it seemed easy but something seemed extremely out of place.

Thoughts lingered in the back of his mind:
"I want to go forward, but there's something holding me back."

Jonah pondered momentarily. The more he reflected on the mission at hand, the more he began to expose the menacing realism of his voyage. There was a faintly distinct bottleneck in this project.

Then slowly it became quite apparent:
"This is a death mission!"

Jonah panicked. Why would God risk sending his own prophet to a pagan country of men that despises His law? These people would never accept salvation and would be extremely reluctant to seek refuge under His everlasting supremacy. How dare God set Jonah up for failure?

The Prophet, looking down at the readily filled bag of essentials, began to rethink what he had signed up for. Jonah realized that the Assyrians did not think highly of the Hebrews nor did they share in Israel's monotheistic beliefs. To travel unexpectedly into enemy territory and tell the Assyrians to stop misbehaving could possibly put him in harm's way. Going as a missionary into a land with a deep culture of unfamiliar religious traditions would probably yield an agonizing death. With these thoughts swirling around his head, suddenly his overnight bag became a suitcase.

Had Jonah existed today, he'd be making arrangements with a moving company, liquidating his assets, and breaking his lease to escape from this arduous duty.

The prophet realized that his enemies would be well within their warped, yet immoral right to kill him. Praying for your enemy is one thing but presenting an argument against them and openly criticizing them, well, that's another.

Discord In Discipleship

The most misunderstood part of our worship life, which often leads to much confusion, is the interpretation of His Word. The most difficult part is following His instructions. It never occurs to the believer that while he or she is asking God, "Which way shall I go?" He is responding, "Which way have I assigned you to go?"

....

HEBREWS 6:10
WAGES OF YOUR WORK
"For God is not unjust to forget your work and labor of love which you have shown toward His name, in that you have ministered to the saints, and do minister."

....

People have a tendency of seeing things in black and white. On the other hand, God is so static that He only gives us His single vision whereas our decisions may produce numerous outcomes. These controls are set beyond the limits of human detection.

Within launching this book, my desire is to minister to the lives of common, ordinary people. You will see in chapters ahead, the subject of this book is as common as we are. I believe in conviction as much as I believe in the responsibility of the Holy Spirit to pilot our godly intentions.

With over thirty, and counting, major Christian groups in existence (along with the four major and five minor Abrahamic faiths across the world) it's understandable how a new believer could become overwhelmed on the path in Christ. We've cluttered the Word of God due to translation and interpretation. Strangely enough, even Non-Denominational has become a denomination. Overall, it is safe to assume with this information that no man is one-hundred percent certain in their understanding of his/her spiritual journey. The only thing we all as a Christian community have agreed on is that God exists and that He has a plan for each of us. How we fit into His plan is analyzed endlessly by scholars and theorists and can be found in the form of the most pondered enigma, "What's the meaning of life?"

People search outwardly, frequently, for a response. We have done so since the birth of civilization. Looking at our own circle of influences we see our family members, friends, and neighbors desperately explore the world looking for entities to help them make sense of life. They find external gratification for a period until they are again dissatisfied. In my own path to discover what God's plan in my life was, I ran into a well-known scripture.

The discipline Matthew, in the sixth chapter of his testament bearing his name, recorded Jesus as saying:

"But seek first his kingdom and his righteousness, and all these

things will be given to you as well."

Decisions In Destiny

The Lord has an amazing way of adding back to us the more we indulge in the gift he has given us. If we are within his will, then nothing can stand in our way.

As previously mentioned, we are often struck with an inventive idea, a jolt of inspiration, or an "ah-ha" moment regarding particular interests. Now motivated, we begin to write our plans out, conduct online research, and even sketch out details of the required work. Thrilled of this grand idea, we guard it tight. Suddenly, after all the stars have aligned, we find ourselves grounded en route due to various obstructions. Maybe it's the lack of funding or certifications needed to get the project off the ground. Soon after we discover these issues we completely drop the idea. We expect it to always be there as we pray for the possibility of suddenly gaining the means to press on. Unsurprisingly, luck usually never comes when we need it most.

Life is the same in this regard. There's a variety of things that deter phases of our individual growth. Of them, fear plays a major role.

Preparedness can debunk fear in most cases. Fear is the most classic feature that can impede success. It grinds against any momentum we have and shatters our shield of confidence.

It is necessary to forecast all things that may stifle our development and challenge our effectiveness as believers. Jesus tells us in Luke 14:25 to "count all costs." We should inspect our inner suspicions, speculations, and skepticisms daily. Similar to exercising, we must train our minds to refute any source where doubt may become malignant.

We must decide and set a clear course. This is not to say that He doesn't care about the intricate details. He has provided the

Believer with the capacity to decide, so it's important to also note that He will not violate the individual's rights or freewill. As long as the decision does not interfere or violate the principle of the demand, the choice may be considered, in most cases, by whichever method we deem suitable.

If He's called you for a task, he has already acknowledged your strengths and is fully aware of your weaknesses. Don't delay or waste time on 'what ifs'. Regardless of how little experience you have or how small your network is, God's grace can help you in your pursuits to create something great.

The Godless Men

Jonah 1:3-5

3 But Jonah arose to flee to Tarshish from the presence of the Lord. He went down to Joppa, and found a ship going to Tarshish; so he paid the fare, and went down into it, to go with them to Tarshish from the presence of the Lord.

4 But the Lord sent out a great wind on the sea, and there was a mighty tempest on the sea, so that the ship was about to be broken up.

5 Then the mariners were afraid; and every man cried out to his god, and threw the cargo that was in the ship into the sea, to lighten the load. But Jonah had gone down into the lowest parts of the ship, had lain down, and was fast asleep.

6 So the captain came to him, and said to him, "What do you mean, sleeper? Arise, call on your God; perhaps your God will consider us, so that we may not perish."

Not much commentary is provided for us to translate throughout this story, which leaves much to speculation. We cannot deny, however, the valuable lessons we receive from what we do know through the recorded scripture. In a timely fashion, the events that led Jonah back toward the path to Nineveh undeniably transpired in sequence to prepare Jonah for the task.

As soon as his doubt had faded, Jonah did not toil about aimlessly. Nor did he sit near an oil lamp at his desk and scribe in fresh ink what he'd say to the people of Nineveh. Instead Jonah, with the putrid smell of digestive fluids and rotten plankton fused to his skin, boldly exclaimed, "Change or die!" Little did he realize the words he was ordered to speak to the Ninevites would be the same verbal charge demanded of him.

The Response to His Plan

So, what's the use of employing a doubtful prophet? Why would God choose an unwilling renegade to confront the idolaters and deliver His message?

It's clear that there's no mentioning of his prior life, education, or trade to validate Jonah as a competent courier of God's Word. We are clueless as to why he was elevated to the honorable status as a prophet. However, we do know this extremely significant fact: Jonah was handpicked for the task at hand. So, if it's good enough for God, then I suppose, he'll do.

When you internalize the meaning of his special appointment we see a broad spectrum of possibilities that give us a tiny window into his life. With this in mind we can link the bits and pieces which are lost within the text. Theoretically speaking, this is the concept behind much of the context of this book: What more is there to learn of Jonah and how can we profit from his ministry?

Of course we all know that God sent Jonah to preach repentance in the land of Nineveh. I believe, in addition to repentance, God sent Jonah to expose their sins. This ordeal would advertently teach Jonah a lesson in submission, which he would later document for generations after him. Although many people consider Jonah's tale as oral fiction, it's unique that this narrative also occurs during an interesting time in the transforming of organized religion.

The scriptures say that Jonah arose and fled to Tarshish in order to escape the presence of the Lord. In his ignorance, the prophet was so dumbfounded at the Lord's request that he absolutely assumed he could sneak away unseen and unscathed. He tried to hide from God. His fear was so great that even his action became erratic. Jonah decided he'd seek citizenship somewhere else just to avoid his calling. Had God continued to turn a blind-eye to the evil in Nineveh, Jonah's fearful response wouldn't have been the deal-breaker for God's mass forgiveness effort. Jonah had briefly forgotten one universal truth - God's plans are bigger than our own.

Unfortunately for the prophet, his task dreadfully needed to be carried out. By running away Jonah not only forfeited his livelihood but he put an entire ship's crew in harm's way.

Acts of Random Selfishness

Think of the sailors and the captain. Think of the families who would be affected due to the tragic loss of their husband, father, brother, etc. who would not return home because of Jonah's disobedience. Since this ship is traveling back to Tarshish it's safe to assume that it is a merchant ship along a trade route. This could mean that there were business owners as well as consumers in Tarshish depending on these men to return safely from Joppa with items they needed to conduct business.

After some time at sea, the Lord sent out a heavy wind. The winds tossed the boat around and waves crashed against it. The worst thing that could happen at sea is inclement weather. This is a threat that most seamen dread. Unfortunately due to the strength of this storm, these men had to dump their bounty. Their cargo and much of their load had to be sacrificed to increase their chances of survival. Little did they know this entire ordeal was all Jonah's fault. Jonah had become a headache not only to God but also to the people he came in contact with. They had been gracious to allow him to travel with them. Sadly, he was a threat to their wellbeing.

It may seem like a stretch but it's important for clarity sake to consider all internal and external individuals directly and indirectly connected to this misadventure. Human travelers and the ship's cargo were insurable assets that needed to return unharmed to the port from where they had originally departed. In addition to the returning freight, other important commodities were being brought back from the land of Israel. The Prophet Jonah put all the cargo, both man and merchandise, in a vulnerable state.

In verse 5, after the ship had entered into the tumultuous storm and much of their items were tossed, the men began to pray. Every man prayed out to his specific god. If that many men prayed to his respective god, there must have been various race and nationalities represented on that boat as well. Obviously they had no knowledge of the True God.

This shows Jonah's failure as the messager. Being a prophet for the Israel nation, Jonah's gift was to inspire his people. I believe Jonah may have had an influential spirit and people enjoyed being around him. He was likely delightful to be around, most times. His very presence demanded respect and more importantly, when he spoke, people listened.

When Praying Goes Wrong

The prophet was being sent to Nineveh to minister to a polytheist, idolatrous people. Had Jonah introduced the sailors to the True Living God of the Hebrews, maybe they could have cried out together immediately at the height of the storm. The fact that they prayed to numerous idol gods may have upset God all the more. The confusion in their scattered worship, along with the roaring thunder overhead, only made matters worse. Oddly enough the commotion was not enough to awaken the prophet who slept below in the ship's lower deck. He did not lose a wink of sleep as the high waters struck the ship on each side.

After the men realized that their prayers were worthless they noticed someone was missing; someone who's prayers had a greater chance to be heard. They were frustrated at the fact that Jonah was sleeping. You have to admit, they had a point, I mean, who could sleep at a time like this?

When they needed Jonah the most, he was nowhere in sight. The captain may have felt a bit disrespected because this was his ship and Jonah had taken advantage of the captain's hospitality. The captain immediately ran down to the lower deck. He urged Jonah to get up and pray to his god. The God of the Hebrews were their last option. They were putting their faith in a god they hadn't known or had a relationship with.

This is a very fascinating moment. Doing what most people do when in distress, these men immediately thought to call on the Lord. Tragically for them the Hebrew prophet was their middleman to a god they had not previously considered. They shouted, "God help us!" but since they had no audience with God, they needed a worthy soul to be an intercessor; a ship chaplain of sorts. Jonah, on the other hand, was not prepared to call on the Lord. Regrettably it was one missed opportunity after another.

MATTHEW 18:18–20
BINDING AGREEMENT

"Again I say to you that if two of you agree on Earth concerning anything that they ask, it will be done for them by My Father in Heaven. For where two or three are gathered together in My name, I am there in the midst of them."

His moment had passed due to his exhaustion, and very possibly a slight case of sea-sickness. He could have helped by sharing the wisdom of God with the men before the storm. Although the storm may not have been avoided, he missed a critical opportunity to save face. Jonah may have possibly gotten a pass from the approaching fate simply by introducing these men to the Creator.

Unfortunately, because he had not demonstrated any role of importance among these gentlemen, he became expendable. Jonah became a liability instead of an asset in this urgent moment. God's headache was increasing.

Missing The Mark

Jonah missed an opportunity to score heavy with God. Not only was he outside of the will of God, he was not thinking clearly. He was so caught up in running away that he neglected all that he was indebted to. Amusingly enough, he was a prophet but had not forecasted his own suffering and self-indulgence. He didn't realize the danger he was inflicting on the company aboard the ship. This trial run of repentance for the Gentile nation was a foreshadow to the coming of Jesus Christ. Had Jonah deviated any longer from his course, it may have possibly affected our relationship with God even today.

Ministering to the non-believer displays the Lord's unbiased love. It also symbolizes the building of His Kingdom here on Earth as a nondiscriminatory establishment. If we are a reflection of his love shouldn't we express this love to our fellow man? Yes, we definitely should.

Utilizing our gifts is essential for the approaching Kingdom of God. It is not easy to see God, especially if one is not aligned with God's will and favor. We are called through our gifts to minister to others who have not yet awakened to the glory that is ancestrally their own through the Holy Spirit.

Grace is free to obtain and has no conditions or contractual obligations in order to be fulfilled. It is our responsibility to show our distressed brothers and sisters the path to the bountiful joy of knowing our Creator and Savior for themselves. Once we understand this as a community of believers, the more we will cast away our judgments and open our hearts to the acceptance of others.

The Reckless Man

Jonah 1:7-9

7 And they said to one another, "Come, let us cast lots that we may know for whose cause this trouble has come upon us." So they cast lots, and the lot fell on Jonah.

8 Then they said to him, "Please tell us! For whose cause is this trouble upon us? What is your occupation? And where do you come from? What is your country? And of what people are you?"

9 So he said to them, "I am a Hebrew; and I fear the Lord, the God of Heaven, who made the sea and the dry land."

Jonah had become a liability. He had all the tools to exceed in his task. Instead he allowed his feelings to dictate his success. Jonah had made the mistake of pocketing God for later use, just as many of us do today.

People tend to believe that God only makes *Himself* available at a certain time or during a particular moment. We have created customs, rituals, and peculiar elicitations in order to invite God into our lives; especially during times of struggle. We petition the Lord and plea our case to Him so that He can move within our various situations. As of late, we find many believers, modern prophets, and charismatic leaders putting on exhibitions to solicit God's attention. So my question is, "Where did God go?"

As of today, there are over 7 billion people atop of this floating rock we call Earth. The Creator of all living things and objects on this planet has the ability to lift anyone out of any situation, at any given time. Do not be mistaken – look at His resume. This is the same God that told Moses to talk to the rock to get the people a sip of water. (Numbers 20:8) He is the same God who tested Job and raised David to the throne of Israel.

The Lord's awareness level is beyond measure. The only thing we can do is pursue God's will, or make the mistake of rejecting it. On the other hand, through our weaknesses and shortcomings, we can present an opportunity for God to appear. When we fall short, God does not dictate how we must suffer. The spiritual realm only responds to the positive or negative circumstances based on our decision-making. At that moment God may arrange the time and place where He can make the most impact.

In theory, Jonah was the Lord's project manager and had the credentials to moderate the entire deliverance mission. He was the vessel used to bring the message of faith and forgiveness to the pagan nation. Jonah subsided however and decided alone how he would spend his potential.

The Ninevite citizens had obviously reached their limit. The Creator was not happy about what was taking place in the town. We can almost bet that the entire land of Assyria was much worse. We discover through the message of love and accountability, God orchestrated the deliverance of Nineveh as an example of what he can do for the entire world. I mean, we Gentiles need love too, right?

If You Got It, Share It

As I continued to explore the sign of which Jesus so eloquently spoke, a noticeable fail in mankind's pursuit of purpose was uncovered. I learned the power in what we've been bestowed and I realized just how long we've squandered it. Commonly our gifts are perverted for self-gratification. We exhibit priority and entitlement in our relationship to the very individuals we are called to serve. Many believers become pompous when they appraise the mortal value of their gifts. They conspire of ways to leverage their heavenly portion to create vainglory opportunities for themselves.

....

1 PETER 4:10
YOUR GIFT TO THE WORLD
"As each one has received a gift, minister it to one another,
as good stewards of the manifold grace of God."

....

Grossing over $67.6 billion worldwide in 2011, the music industry is one of the highest revenue grossing businesses. Christian/Gospel album sales represented roughly 6% of the overall sales. That's a huge difference. The biggest difference is in the messages that are being transmitted to our minds and feeding our consciences. Many artists spend their aesthetic gifts by disrespecting authority, women, their communities, and themselves. Others choose to use their voices to honor the Creator.

What we have is not ours to hoard simply for material gain. Worship artists know that their voices, the musical arrangements, and words belong to The Creator and they make it their business to showcase their gift for the world of believers to enjoy.

The further I meditated and visualized within the chapter I could see the self-determined ex-prophet making his way up the stairs leading to the ship's deck. Little did Jonah know his independence would be short-lived. Successfully evading the task at hand, he clicks his heels, pays his fare, then seeks out the captain to secure his place among the crew. As the captain comes over to him, Jonah may have used his appointment as a ploy to board a merchant ship. Anyone could have paid a toll to get aboard but not everyone longing for a voyage to Tarshish was a prophet. Only knowing his career as a prophet, we can assume his prestige allowed for any preferential treatment Jonah received while en route to Tarshish. Denying Jonah, a Hebrew prophet, would not serve as a hospitable gesture and could very well be bad for business.

Joppa, now modern-day Tel Aviv, was a well-established port city. I can imagine from a bird's eye view, this bustling town with miles of undisturbed woodlands fading abruptly into clusters of square, mortar structures. Beyond the compact, ancient urban metropolis rests a busy, blue Mediterranean coast. One area reserved for summertime beach activities and the other for shipping and receiving. It's where countless logistical transactions take place. Joppa serves as the premier hub for international trade and distribution for much of the Middle East and North Africa.

Under Jeroboam II, Israel continues to grow in prominence and influence. The dynamic of Hebrew life was changing with the time. Although free trade hadn't helped to preserve the spiritual identity of the nation, it created a significant economical bump. The Kingdoms of Israel and Judah were gradually diversifying and were experiencing cultures and customs of worlds beyond their borders. Having a dense population meant consistent business and fresh shipments from Tarshish and other influential cities along the Mediterranean coast.

The captain, seeing a Hebrew leader in front of him, may not have wanted this man to travel on his ship. The God of the Hebrew religion, nor the law of their forefathers, had yet gained crossover notoriety. Nevertheless, he was well aware of what "the cloth" represented to his Israelite clientele.

He must have known the sacred relationship the Hebrews had with the God of their ancestors. It would not be a good business practice to disrespect or anger a man who embodied their unified symbol of deliverance and strength. The captain had a difficult decision to make. Imagine if the Pope knocked on your door and requested a warm bed for a few days, would you allow him to enter?

Jonah, fully aware of his influence, used his position to gain access where he was otherwise, unwelcomed. Winning the captain's apprehensive approval, Jonah expressed his gratitude and made himself at home. To keep an eye on Jonah, he may have advised him to stay below deck. He kept Jonah safe inside an empty cabin. Knowing the caliber and habits of the free-spirited, loose-lipped men he had employed as shipmates, the captain did not want to expose the prophet, the man of God, to such behavior. Jonah would cause no harm or get in the way. The captain probably thought of Jonah as his very own good luck charm. Prepped and ready, he calls out to the crew so they can begin their course across the sea.

Waste Not, Want Not

The Prophet Jonah committed an extreme foul. He had now piled one disrespectful action atop another. It was not enough to flee God's command. Jonah "upped the ante" and used God's gift of power and position to secure his way aboard a merchant ship. He would soon discover that his actions would put him and the entire crew in harm's way.

When we occupy God's favor in a way that glorifies us, it displeases Him. We are here to serve Him, not ourselves. There is nothing wrong about accepting rewards from those willing to extend their appreciativeness.

....

HEBREWS 6:10
WAGES OF YOUR WORK

"For God is not unjust to forget your work and labor of love which you have shown toward His name, in that you have ministered to the saints, and do minister."

....

Gift-giving is unquestionably an authentic form of love. Yet it is when the believer expects something in return for the use of their spiritual gifts, or when the benefits of those gifts are elaborately displayed, that is the moment it breaches the thin line between humility and ego.

If we work ceaselessly within the will of God, he will undoubtedly supply our needs. The time and energy we sacrifice toward the complete manifestation of God's purpose will not return to us void. It is not necessary to expect anything from anyone. Only expect your due compensation according to God's eternal promise. Any rank, title, or professional designation you have been given in this world means very little to The Creator.

We must make a conscious effort to ensure that our position does not affect the condition upon which we maintenance our gift.

What you have is awesome! Be proud of the favor He has over your life, but do not indulge in it recklessly.

The Man In Distress

Jonah 1:10-16

10 Then the men were exceedingly afraid, and said to him, "Why have you done this?" For the men knew that he fled from the presence of the Lord, because he had told them.

11 Then they said to him, "What shall we do to you that the sea may be calm for us?"—for the sea was growing more tempestuous.

12 And he said to them, "Pick me up and throw me into the sea; then the sea will become calm for you. For I know that this great tempest is because of me."

13 Nevertheless the men rowed hard to return to land, but they could not, for the sea continued to grow more tempestuous against them.

14 Therefore they cried out to the Lord and said, "We pray, O Lord, please do not let us perish for this man's life, and do not charge us with innocent blood; for You, O Lord, have done as it pleased You."

15 So they picked up Jonah and threw him into the sea, and the sea ceased from its raging.

16 Then the men feared the Lord exceedingly, and offered a sacrifice to the Lord and took vows

Jonah's bad luck came as a result of his unwillingness to go preach in Nineveh. It was far more than the storm that forced him overboard. Jonah had made some pretty poor choices immediately after leaving his home. Oddly enough the farther he sailed away from the shore the closer he came in eyeshot of the Lord.

His "stay-cation" inside of the stomach of the creature is certainly a debate worthy conundrum. Be it an actual event or ancient Hebrew lore, the tale serves as a forewarning of our inability to explore our own potential.

At various stages of life we can relate to taking a bold leap forward then stepping backward to reach for a support net. Sadly for many of us that support net can be an addiction, bad habit, or reconnecting with another reckless person. The testament of Jonah doesn't discuss the particulars, but it's depressing to seeing how Jonah accepted this cruel fate without giving himself a fighting chance. Anxiety had given way. He became somber and ready to give up. At this point he could think of only one way to gain some peace and attempt to sort out the mess he got himself into. Jonah suggested that they kill him so that he could be taken out of his misery.

Before he was tossed into the ocean grave, there was a brief conversation between the men. Each sailor had already done all they could do to save themselves. Crates, barrels, and other supplies were thrown overboard to lighten the load of the ship. This did nothing for the might of the wind and water threatening to break the ship apart. Calling upon their individual deities, they hoped for salvation; another ineffective means.

Death To Excellence

After the men had done all the obvious things to ensure the safety of the ship Jonah intervened. He came clean about how he'd come to join them aboard the ship. Though tremendously furious with Jonah's dishonesty, the men instantly realized the power of the God of the Hebrews. The very god whom they had not previously acknowledged had focused his wrath upon them. Jonah confirmed the next step they must take to save themselves. He said, "Pick me up and throw me into the sea; then the sea will become calm for you..."

They were reluctant to leave him stranded in such a terrible environment. They immediately pleaded their innocence and asked to not be held responsible for their part in the pending homicide; the obvious outcome of Jonah's deceptive behavior.

The men cast lots to see which would be thrown overboard next - more profit, or the prophet. They literally flipped a coin to see which deserved to be spared.

....

JOHN 19:23-24
LUCK WITHDRAWN

"Then the soldiers, when they had crucified Jesus, took His garments and made four parts, to each soldier a part, and also the tunic....They said therefore among themselves, "Let us not tear it, but cast lots for it, whose it shall be..."

....

The shipmates, on the other hand, had no pleasure in taking a life. It was a generous gesture, although Jonah had made it very clear that he was the cause of the storm. We should know by now that Lady Luck is not the friend of desperate measures. Therefore, Jonah met his demise at the roll of the die. But then again, he had already gambled his life away.

Together they lifted the prophet and tossed him into the sea. They waited and peered over the ledge as Jonah struggled to stay afloat. Once they executed Jonah's wishes, they cried out to God for forgiveness. Each sailor searched his heart. God eased the tempest, thus displaying his authority over their tribulation. They were uncomfortable with their cruelty yet somehow vindicated in the "necessary evil" they had carried out.

The Lord not only presented control over the storm, but also over human life. This encounter caused them to receive the Lord as their own and they offered a sacrifice to Him. At Jonah's expense the men saw firsthand what a broken faith life can produce. Faith in the Creator could achieve miraculous benefits. The lack of faith, however, can cause destructive circumstances.

Although the men accepted the Lord and prayed unto him for His saving grace, Jonah still failed to acknowledge God. I can't help but to think, "What if Jonah had prayed right there on the top deck of the ship?"

As the wind rocked the boat and rain broke against his brow, Jonah could have repented and requested that the storm be made still. The Lord provoked a verbal relationship with Jonah when he ordered him to go to Nineveh. This could mean that he had open, vocal communication with the Creator. So, why didn't he speak to the storm? Then again, why did *he* not pray?

Jonah orchestrated his own demise by prompting the seamen to throw him overboard. He took the easy way out when in a moment's notice he could have fallen to his knees and pleaded for the safety of them all. It's sad knowing how his disobedience brought an impending demise on those onboard with him. These men were ensnared in a mess that could have been avoided.

Don't Look Down

Turn on your television. The news is filled with heartfelt stories of people who have fallen on hard times and claimed to have no way out. Sadly, many of those people extinguish their lives too soon. For youth ages 15 to 24, suicide is the third leading cause of death. Our youth are murdering their potential by giving up too soon. According to data compiled by the World

Health Organization, suicide is the 10th leading cause of death in the United States. In 2009, the total number of suicides reached 36,909.

The data also shows that suicide is the 7th leading cause of death for men. It's a personal tragedy and gutless act. It also creates severe implications on the loved ones who are left to deal with such a lost.

Just think if these individuals had waited a second longer, even a day later. If only they had given themselves a fighting chance. Author Robert H. Schuller states in his bestselling book that "Tough times never last, but tough people do." The first thing that appears in the summary of this publication is a compelling message that states, "Name your problem, and you name your possibility."

There was once a time when we had to take cameras to a photo lab to get them developed. Remember that? After they were done you'd get home and reach into the envelope to look at your pictures. Accompanying those colorful snapshots of our precious moments was a set of black-tinted strips. If you didn't know, or were too young to recall, those were the negatives.

A photo was unable to be developed without the negatives. Likewise, we cannot expect and appreciate the good in life without enduring the menacing, dark moments. Green Bay Packers Head Coach Vince Lombardi was quoted as saying, "The difference between a successful person and others is not a lack of strength, not a lack of knowledge, but rather a lack in will."

It's an injustice to our families, friends, and even to humanity, to disrupt any opportunity for your purpose to thrive. God has given us a portion of strength that should be activated to the highest degree especially when we fall into the lowest point in our lives. Regardless of what problems life brings, it is not the end. For the sake of your purpose, look deep within to find the strength needed to pick yourself up and turn those negatives into a positive picture.

The Dead Man Sinking

Jonah 2: 3-6

3 You hurled me into the depths, into the very heart of the seas, and the currents swirled about me; all your waves and breakers swept over me.

4 I said, I have been banished from your sight; yet I will look again toward your holy temple.

5 The engulfing waters threatened me, the deep surrounded me; seaweed was wrapped around my head.

6 To the roots of the mountains I sank down; the earth beneath barred me in forever. But you, Lord my God, brought my life up from the pit.

Even now, in authoring a book based on Jonah's adventure to Nineveh, a part of me feels as though the biographer exaggerated the prophet's tale a tad bit.

I must admit that it's pretty difficult for my mind to comprehend a whale, or large fish, devouring a human. Moreover, it's tough to imagine a human actually escaping to tell of the experience. Now, by no means am I abandoning the opportunity for a miraculous event like this to take place. Clearly there's a valuable lesson to be gained from this story. In the case of its authenticity, being validated by various ancient scribing and documentation, I am inclined to accept it as a true historical event.

The fact that it is compiled among other God-inspired works ensures that there must exist some reflective meaning between each sentence.

My real issue is with the author. The prophet hasn't really painted a picture of himself as being a standup guy. All things considered, what've we learned so far? Well, we know that he was a self-centered, very unreliable, and stubborn gentleman. I must also mention that he was very resourceful; especially when it cames to getting what he wanted.

It's not an impossible thing to find ourselves in unbecoming situations like Jonah had. The ramifications of our disobedience can manifest themselves in some pretty bizarre ways. Moving forward, my analytical mind will delve a bit deeper into the scene that takes place somewhere adrift the turbulent Mediterranean Sea.

Life At A Glance

The day we are born the universe immediately launches a timeline for us. Instantaneously our first breath becomes as significant as our last. The whale not only represents a probable resting place for the prophet, it also confirms the inescapability of death for each of us.

For three days Jonah was away from the face of God. Grievously, this is exactly what he wanted. His intention was to escape God and bury any trace of his purpose and his past. The biggest disappointment was in his thinking that he could get away with running away. But Death is not ours to dictate.

....

JOHN 10:17-18
POWER OVER DEATH

"Therefore My Father loves Me, because I lay down My life that I may take it again. No one takes it from Me, but I lay it down of Myself. I have power to lay it down, and I have power to take it again. This command I have received from My Father."

....

When we get outside of God's will we leave ourselves vulnerable to whatever unpleasant result this world can administer. Although the world offers many attractive objects and options to experience, we should not lose sight of the very short time our physical presence exists on this planet. The frailty of life is oftentimes not considered when we make erroneous decisions. We put ourselves in jeopardy by refusing a life of service and purpose through Jesus Christ. We can never overcome death. It is inevitable and it will come as is determined by the One who created us.

As precious as life is, it is also very brief. There are graveyards across the globe that are full of men and women who chose to forfeit their divine potential and spiritual gifts. These individuals fled from the greatness within and separated themselves from their purpose. They surrendered themselves to moments of ungodliness and unfulfilling desires. They defined vanity as joy and materialism as happiness. Many of us find ourselves enslaved to any and every facet of this worldly existence. Honestly, we are all guilty of it at some point.

There's nothing you can own or acquire that can provide more value to your life than grace. No amount of money can buy you away from God's love. And though we trade time for money at our respective places of employment, no position or title earned can supersede the favor that God has placed inside you. Before your life is extinguished, how will you dispense your potential?

Die Trying

I'd also like to point out that the sea creature serves as the prime participant in Jonah's counterproductive behavior. The prophet put himself in harm's way therefore harm gravitated toward him. He sinned by violating God's command and chose to disobey His orders. According to the Apostle Paul, the wages of sin is death. (Romans 6:23) If the whale represents death then it is safe to say, especially from a biblical standpoint, that Death is the enemy.

In the formation of the Earth, death was not a concern. Death was not a threat to mankind nor was it considered the opposite of Life. God created man to experience this world as an external eternity. When mankind fell Death was introduced into the natural order – rather Death was initiated as a circumstance of Adam and Eve's *disobedience*.

The dark of death looms even more today. It is not our ally. It works against us at every conscious moment. Death separates us from our body and from our families.

....

PHILIPPIANS 1:23-25
WHY YOU CANNOT DIE

"For I am hard-pressed between the two, having a desire to depart and be with Christ, which is far better. Nevertheless to remain in the flesh is more needful for you....I shall remain and continue with you all for your progress and joy of faith."

....

For the believer, it prevents our work from being accomplished. On the other hand, if one is not covered in the faith, it can forever separate a man's soul from God into a *Christ-less* eternity.

Christ has conquered death so we can rest assured that our good works will not fade away with our last breath. Jesus claimed the authority over Death. Since we are the heirs to God's Kingdom we can rest likewise be confident in His authority over our lives. Henceforth, our sights should remain focused on our work.

In his weakness Jonah's near death experience exposed an ignorance developing in many people today. We must deny ourselves daily in order to not lose ourselves to the daily trials and complexities of this world. The Word of God tells us that the sting of death has been swallowed up in the victory of Christ. Before we were born God gave our lives meaning, a purpose. Therefore we should seize each moment to assess our spiritual endurance and forward the cause that God has predetermined for each human on this planet.

As a believer, take into account that the bigger your purpose is, the more you will suffer. In the next chapter you will discover how Jonah ultimately realized this important factor regarding his servitude to God. I am confident that his words serve as encouragement for us all. Be it large or small, he challenges us to be results-driven in our daily purpose-filled lives.

The Praying Man

Jonah 2: 1-10

1 Then Jonah prayed to the Lord his God from the fish's belly.

2 And he said: "I cried out to the Lord because of my affliction, and He answered me...

7 "When my soul fainted within me, I remembered the Lord; And my prayer went up to You, Into Your holy temple.

8 "Those who regard worthless idols forsake their own Mercy.

9 But I will sacrifice to You With the voice of thanksgiving; I will pay what I have vowed. Salvation is of the Lord."

10 So the Lord spoke to the fish, and it vomited Jonah onto dry land.

It's not a coincidence that the entire second chapter of *The Book of Jonah* is a simple prayer. The first chapter covered a few examples of how the prophet tried to ditch his destiny. Jonah disclosed the various errors he made. He had time to contemplate over his mistakes for the first two days inside of the fish. The second chapter occurs on the third day he's trapped at sea.

Visualize the situation:

The light from an orange moon ripples across the ocean's current. Evening had come. With only an inch of life remaining and minutes of tainted oxygen stretching thin, Jonah realizes enough is enough. He begins to focus and breathe from a generous yet foul pocket of air as he utters a sincere prayer to God. The prayer is as open and honest as any death bed prayer could be. Thinking back, this prayer is one that he should have been prayed earlier while in the company of the seamen; possibly even as he looked out to the sea from the shoreline in Joppa. Jonah lifts a prayer of admiration and thanksgiving to the Lord. The raging storm had certainly warranted such a dynamic plea. Jonah figures a prayer was better late than never.

Power Of Prayer

Jonah zealously sought God's attention. After leaning to his own understanding, and after being tried and denied, the prophet anxiously comes back to the Lord.

He had stumbled and landed himself in a worse off place than any heathen city imaginable. For his life's sake, Jonah sets his ego aside and consults God. It was obvious that he needed help. Instead of stating the obvious, Jonah declared to God that he would complete his task.

He had left his home, wasted time and money aboard the ship, but most of all he had lost his way. With this in mind, Jonah revised his strategy and revisited his salvation. It was evidently the only thing he had left; the only thing he couldn't lose. He should have been dead at this point. God had kept him alive in the most horrific place one could be in. Yet through it all the prophet exhibits a reinforced conviction for God's original plan. After all the things he had done to rattle his faith, he still found it logical to reach out to his Creator.

I believe that it was Jonah's objective to devote the entire second chapter of his book to show us the power of an earnest prayer. In many aspects this prayer has the makings of a psalm. Relatively speaking, Jonah's petition fitted into the standard that mimics the *23rd Psalm* of King David. As David was tucked away hidden from the murderous envy of King Saul, he wrote of God's omniscience. The Creator is likewise exalted through Jonah's submissive prayer.

When dealing with abductions or missing person's cases, the first 48 hours are the most stringent. All the leads are gathered, regional authorities are alerted, and parameters are being set in order to find the individual who has suddenly vanished. Two entire days at sea had passed and the opportunity of a successful recovery for the Hebrew prophet was beginning to fade.

God's enduring presence is a noteworthy motif in Jonah's prayer. He says, "because of my affliction…" which implies that he went through serious mental torment.

In verse 3, Jonah acknowledged that he was at fault. He says that God *casted* him into the deep but he wasn't blaming God for his misery. The prophet is merely presenting the manner by which God had compounded the risks he took beyond the damage that he had done. Even in his agonizing state, Jonah shows his reverence to, as well as the magnitude of, God's glory.

He hypothetically spoke of what was taking place outside of the digestive tract of the beast. He goes as far as describing the depths of the sea although he is unable to see plainly around him. It's amazing how he mentions parts of the Earth at depths that mankind had not charted; not until the most recent century. Either way, he claims that he had traveled to the mountains heel. Jonah states that the earth, or presence of a visible land mass, was far behind him. This denotes that the beast had plunged miles below the Earth's surface during the two days. At these depths it is possible that the atmospheric pressure may have caused Jonah some mild decompression sickness. He confidently assumed his time had come. As a result he had admittedly accepted death as his fate. From this perspective, the possibility for redemption, or rescue, looked bleak.

Despite the fact that he was far removed from any familiar setting, Jonah found prayer to be the answer. He confidently called upon the creator of all of Earth's foundations for deliverance. The prophet was secure in the Lord's authority over life and death. He did not have to do anything special while in this moment of distress. Jonah was confident that, if anything, God would find him through his humble prayer.

You're In Good Hands

The Bible tells us that God does perceive all things, which means that neither thought nor undertaking can be hidden from His knowledge. King David recognized, "Indeed, the darkness shall not hide from You, but the night shines as the day; the darkness and the light are both alike to You." (Psalm 139:12)

God sees all things, even the hidden things. The secret intentions of our hearts are closely monitored because of His interest in our lives. In fact, He understands our own intentions better than we do. This explains the mercy that was offered to Jonah. Even as he casually toured the sea inside of the beast, God's mercy was transforming the instrument of his demise into the vehicle that would take him back to dry land. Though it may appear to be a farfetched method to get His point across, you have to admit it's a unique way for God's magnificent sovereignty to take form.

It's important to note that *The Book of Jonah* is one of the few Old Testament records showing the God of the Hebrews extending his compassion to outsiders. Jonah had failed to see how important he was to the movement that was taking place. In the case of Jonah, God was merely protecting his investment.

Jonah was confined to his own insolence and ultimately possessed the key to his own liberation. Had Jonah not been girded in heavenly favor, he might have found himself inside of a creature with a carniverous appetite instead. Likewise, had grace not been extended on his behalf, there is a high probability that he could've drowned and been lost at sea forever.

Prayer was the only thing that had been missing the entire time. Imagine if he had prayed sooner. Just as doubt crept into his mind he could have possibly avoided much of this pointless suffering. I'm not saying it was all in vain, but his problems could have been easily avoided had he prayed initially. It would have given him the strength needed to power forward. Praying through his fear would have given him the reassurance of knowing God would be with him the entire way. At this point, the prophet realized that day and night had lapsed and, ironically, he was still alive. This was a pivotal moment in his faith simply because he remembered how miracles are birthed. Miraculous breakthroughs opt to arrive as soon as we hand over our last dollar, cry our last tear, and spill our last drop of hope.

Human beings perceive through the senses, but there are limits to what the senses let us perceive and understand. I'm grateful that God's senses are not limited like ours.

HEBREWS 4:13
IN PLAIN SIGHT OF GOD
"And there is no creature hidden from His sight, but all things are naked and open to the eyes of Him to whom we must give account."

His Spirit searches all things and nothing is beyond his perception. As Paul explains, "there is no creature hidden from His sight, but all things are naked and open to the eyes of Him to whom we must give account".

Preventing mistakes in our life is easier said than done. Our decisions can sometimes cause us to fall outside of God's plan. Regardless how many times we fall, we can never be outside of God's glory. His forgiveness is infinite but we have to remain conscious of ways we can improve. By picking up our cross we pledge to walk with Jesus, even if it means to suffer. When we prolong heaven's desire for our lives, we find ourselves wandering aimlessly in the world. By indulging in prayer and supplication, the believer can build confidence in even the most merciless situations.

Don't Just Pray, Participate!

With faith at its base, prayer is an ingredient that can spark explosive results in our lives. The impact of faith in our lives is essential to developing one's individual ministry. I look at my ministry as if it's a business. I own my gift. Believers and unbelievers alike are my customers. I conduct my business in various ways, as long as the end result is me being a blessing to my clients. I am employed through the Holy Spirit and I am contracted under divine administration. I am often inspired by people and many have come in my life to assist me when I'm having issues or seasons of low productivity. My overall goal is to work ambitiously to align myself with God's plan and to cultivate a lasting legacy of faith. The best part is that it costs me absolutely nothing to provide my service. Fortunate for me I don't have any bookkeeping responsibilities. No receipts or purchase orders are mandated to be filed or submitted. When in need, I simply pray to my boss and in turn he supplies my needs - according to his riches and glory. (Philippians 4:19)

Heaven has standard operating procedures that we must, at all times, be in line with. In the past when using my gift to pursue my own personal interests, like the Prophet Jonah, I found myself in a jam. It doesn't take long before I fall on my knees praying for an escape or for redirection. In most cases, even in my selfish acts, I usually gain a valuable lesson. This has however increased my faith and my spiritual durability. What has ensued from a life of mishaps and disorder is an authentic, devoted man who continues daily to search for God's heart.

It's extremely important that we stay anchored in the commandments of God. We must move when he says so. Instead of praying our way out of trouble, we should being each day praying for God to renew our senses so that we can hear Him and follow His direction.

Notice the last sentence of Jonah's prayer. He honored God's plan and his role in the mission. Jonah made amends by saying, "I will pay what I have vowed." The prophet says that he'll keep his promise. Jonah was also reminded that God has trusted him with this gift and he was obligated to pay back what he owed to the Lord.

What is it that we owe? We owe all we have – everything! It's more than just our songs, our praise, or ten percent of our gross earnings. That's not enough; that's only the minimum of what He will honor. Clearly these minor sacrifices are a test of our obedience. At some extent we must pay Him with our life through service to others and faithfully adhere to his commandments.

Our Creator manifests his power through man therefore the believer must always acknowledge Him in all stages of decision making. Our daily prayer should be for strength that will enable us to move forward, not when it is convenient to us, but when it is appropriate for God.

The Man With A Purpose

Jonah 3:1-4

1 Now the word of the Lord came to Jonah the second time, saying,
2 "Arise, go to Nineveh, that great city, and preach to it the message
that I tell you."
3 So Jonah arose and went to Nineveh, according to the word of
the Lord. Now Nineveh was an exceedingly great city, a three-day
journey in extent.
4 And Jonah began to enter the city on the first day's walk. Then
he cried out and said, "Yet forty days, and Nineveh shall be
overthrown!"

Like most children, my parents imposed a strict bedtime on me growing up. My parents sent me to bed each night promptly at 10 o'clock p.m. Tired or not, I had to be in my rooms, in the bed, and all lights had to be out. Relaxing in the den, my mom would pull a basket of wrinkled clothes near the couch, draw the coffee table close to her and switch channels on television. At the time, one of her favorite shows was in syndication. I could faintly hear the show's theme music and introduction from my bedroom, "...boldly go where no man has gone before." Upset that I couldn't watch it, I imagined the iconic scene of the Starship Enterprise blast into the unknown wildernesses of space and time.

So far we know that Jonah had lodged inside of the intestines of the sea creature for three days. Now it would take him three days more to reach Nineveh. Going to Nineveh would pose as a challenge. Crossing the various terrain of the Middle Eastern landscape would give him the time get his bearings and focus on the next stage of the journey. He had to make the most of the trip since his resources where limited. All of his possessions were possibly sold off or thrown overboard with him. Nonetheless, with his thoughts and assumptions far behind, Jonah enthusiastically continued forward. His sights were set on the path ahead. Unsure of what was beyond, Jonah's only expectation was for God to move through him. His determination and renewed faith gave him the driving spirit he needed to complete the assignment before him. As he approached the city gates on the last day of his journey, Jonah had no time to rest or relax.

Going was only the first phase of the operation. Proclaiming God's word would be the next step in completing the provisional obligation. Nineveh was no small town. It was massive. The text doesn't give an approximate measurement of the perimeter of the city, instead it recalls the amount of days it took to go through it.

Day One

He had arrived inside the city gates and immediately began interacting with the rival nation. Jonah fearlessly foretold of the event that would occur if they did not avert from their wickedness. Men and women alike accepted his words as truth and followed his instruction. From the city gates at day to the city's interior, the Prophet Jonah would begin his entire afternoon ministering to the lost.

Day Two

The next day he traveled from the interior to the central district of Nineveh – downtown. He stayed true to the same script and procedures that he had initiated the day before. Their undivided attention was focused on to this odd, yet charismatic, Hebrew man. According to God's lecture to Jonah found in Chapter 4, over 100,000 Ninevites humbled themselves to his words.

Jonah did not waste any time. He was determined to get in and get out. There was no need to prolong the inevitable. The city was set to be destroyed and he didn't want to be there when "all Heaven" broke loose.

Jonah witnessed the way they lived and how the Ninevites managed their daily lives. They were regular people, flesh and blood. Their principals and customs, as dissimilar as they were to him, seemed to increase his passion to spawn change within this uncivil land. It was a message they needed to hear. This was not for entertainment purposes, rather this was for survival.

Day Three

Word of his message spread as day fell and sat on the minds of the Ninevites as Jonah had slept. The third day of his citywide rendezvous would be much like the two prior. His popularity and influence had preceded him, making his presence an anticipated engagement. The people along the last leg of his trip were primed and were anxious to hear what he had to say.

At dawn Jonah began to assemble a crowd. His lecture was as dynamic as it was the first day he had arrived. The people fell to their knees fully immersed in the glory of God through the testament of Jonah. They had faith in their hearts and change on their minds. Their entire attitude had been adjusted. There was but one person left to deliver the message to, the king of Nineveh.

Seeing this religious man, the symbol of Israel's faith, could have given the Assyrians some serious leverage to make some pretty steep demands. It's no secret that the neighboring country was in relentless conflict with the Kingdom of Israel. By the time he had reached the palace, Jonah's reputation may have put him on Assyria's "Most Wanted" list.

Prophet Jonah made it to the palace gates and is recognized as an enemy. Soldiers drew their weapons, arrested Jonah, and immediately delivered him into the hands of the King. Jonah, weary from the journey, hadn't the strength to fight. Once more he was accosted by a group of men seeking to build a case against him. This time his only plan was to share the divine message, one last time, and leave the soon to be damned city.

The Royal Reply

The King sees a small group of guards coming towards his courtyard. Those not as receptive to his apocalyptic words taunt him and throw objects at the acclaimed prophet. Bystanders gasp at the sight of Jonah. They are uncertain of who the prophet is but notice his distinct appearance. The skin of the Hebrew man was slightly disfigured from stomach bile (the smell of which faintly lingers in his clothing).

As the messenger was chaperoned to the steps of the palace

he's tossed into the court to stand before a royal judge.

....

MATTHEW 10:16-20
THRONE OF JUDGEMENT

"Behold, I send you out as sheep in the midst of wolves...You will be brought before governors and kings for My sake...it will be given to you in that hour what you should speak; for it is not you who speak, but the Spirit of your Father who speaks in you."

....

The King peers over to the prophet and settles into his seat. Without a waning sprite of fear, Jonah moves in closer. Both men gaze at the other; the King draped in regal fashion clouded over in expensive fragrance and Jonah wrapped in shabby strips of cheap fabric and reeking of decomposed plankton. There is no introduction nor does Jonah greet the King. Jonah, eager to break the chilling silence says, "Forty more days and Nineveh will be overthrown!"

The audacity of Jonah! The nerve of him to talk to the king in such a manner!

What's compelling is that even in Jonah's mental, physical, and spiritual anguish, God sought an opportunity to bless him. After recovering his servant from the out of the ocean, he instilled something new into Jonah. Fearlessness not only helped Jonah to finish the course but it also allowed him to speak openly and honestly to the king. The very message of destruction would be one he could relate to personally. He now felt an obligation to tell the people of the severe activity of their faith.

The same message he had delivered the previous days were the exact words he would say to the king. He did not veer from what had worked previously, nor did he alter the word of God to cater it to the king. The fact is, Jonah's message was not one shaped in kindness, unity, or coddled sympathy; quite the contrary. His words vowed death and destruction upon the King and his people. He spoke only of the hazardous outcome they would suffer if they failed to activate their faith in God through repentance.

A Beacon of Change

Clearly Jonah sets the example for us to follow. Once we have reached the gates of our destiny we must exhibit efficiency and confidence in the moment. I can imagine Jonah being concerned about a number of things but he never let the Ninevites see him sweat. His appearance, how the people would receive him, and the opinions of others could have deterred him from his objective. However, he did not stray from what he was given. He had a second chance to make things right. Although his outer appearance was not up to par, Jonah kept pace and wielded optimism throughout the city.

Following Jonah's example, we learn that to create change we must first change ourselves. We must challenge our individual way of thinking. Only by doing so can we discover the limitations we set on ourselves. As believers we must learn to lead while at the same time not block the blessings of others. God has provided us with a road map. Within each of us is a gift that we must use to complete His plans.

There are so many people that are hurt and in distress. The cause of the believer is standing before the world with the solution to remedy these issues. We are called to assist, encourage, and bless the lost by boldly proclaiming the love of God and to work within His vision for the world.

The Man of Authority

Jonah 3:1-4

5 So the people of Nineveh believed God, proclaimed a fast, and put on sackcloth, from the greatest to the least of them.

6 Then word came to the king of Nineveh; and he arose from his throne and laid aside his robe, covered himself with sackcloth and sat in ashes.

7 And he caused it to be proclaimed and published throughout Nineveh by the decree of the king and his nobles, saying, Let neither man nor beast, herd nor flock, taste anything; do not let them eat, or drink water.

8 But let man and beast be covered with sackcloth, and cry mightily to God; yes, let everyone turn from his evil way and from the violence that is in his hands.

9 Who can tell if God will turn and relent, and turn away from His fierce anger, so that we may not perish? 10 Then God saw their works that they turned from their evil way; and God relented from the disaster that He had said He would bring upon them, and He did not do it."

Thankfully the Prophet Jonah's words did not fall on death ears. He proclaimed the word of God and within the first day of his visit many of the people accepted him. Jonah's enthusiasm had spread throughout the city and this momentum would continue all the way to the royal palace.

The Road Less Traveled

Whenever we work wholeheartedly within our gift amazing things can happen. The fears that we had suddenly vanish. The excuses we make seem so silly and the people who called us fools look to us for mercy. Initially Jonah predicted that the people would laugh at him and give him grief. Death undoubtedly came into his mind as a possible outcome. However, after surviving a three-day prison sentence inside of the gigantic sea creature there was absolutely nothing that could shake him.

PSALMS 119:15-16
MEDITATE ON GOD'S WORD
"I will meditate on Your precepts, And contemplate Your ways.
I will delight myself in Your statutes; I will not forget Your word."

What in this world could possibly top being stranded inside of a whale? My guess would be – nothing. The fear of a human person couldn't hold a candle to being trapped, literally, within the belly of the beast. Jonah, seemingly fearless at this point, no longer feared the thought of death, embarrassment, or awkwardness.

I sincerely hope that we do not experience immoveable, unyielding faith in the manner that Jonah had. The prophet's faith had blossomed from being put in an extremely preposterous place. He was instructed to be in one location but his doubts lead him elsewhere. Due to his replacing faith with fear, he found himself in a position that he hadn't intended on being.

Learning from Jonah's example, there should be no reason for us to doubt the plan that God has. Neither should we live our lives afraid of the potential, within us, he has most graciously supplied.

The Masterpiece

I began drawing and painting abruptly after my escape from the womb. As I began to develop into a school-aged child, words seemed to help me release my thoughts in a way that others could understand. I was the kind of child with a huge imagination and, in my mind, nothing was impossible. Even today I still feel this way; albeit my imagination is a bit more refined.

One day, after studying the "Creation Story", it came to me. God created man from dust, a billion tiny granules. As I reflected on this I considered the fact that many scientific terms had not yet been invented. Maybe at that time the author of the book of Genesis (scholars claim Moses) had no word for molecules, so he used dust to describe them. Well, within each of these particles God inserted a much smaller compound, DNA. Without it there could be no lineage and, furthermore, we could have no identity to claim.

God's imagination wowed me yet again. In the great celestial spaces of his mind, God imagined you and I. He started with the smallest component of life and built upon it. Then, as he breathed life into the masterpiece, he knighted you with a purpose and sealed a gift to your soul. That gift is your product and it is your responsibility to share with the rest of us.

Faith through Christ means that anything can happen. Jesus gives an analogy regarding a mustard seed to explain how, with even the smallest dose of faith, a situation can be turned around. (Luke 17) Unfiltered faith can also alter the course of history. The Ninevites had faith in the words of Jonah; so much so, they changed. They knew that their ways were wrong but society had made it comfortable for them to wallow in sin. Are we any different?

Think of all the things we have adjusted our principles around. Think of the images we glorify and expose ourselves to daily. Images of violence, vulgar behavior, drugs, etc. are the topic of every media outlet. We can hardly enjoy simple things like listening to the radio, watching television programs, or films without the effort of filtering them. Parents are encouraged frequently to screen videos, music, and games before purchasing them for their kids.

The Ninevites had no customs and had adopted destructive lifestyles. They lived life openly. Since they had not subdued their many passions nor held accountable for inappropriate activities, they became deprived of restraint and empathy. Imagine their shame and concern when Jonah shouted of the jeopardy they were in. The entire mass of townspeople immediately came to the realization that their fun and excitement had all been in vain.

Nothing good had come of their frequent drunkenness and sexually-charged festivals. It was time to change and after hearing Jonah's blunt message, change was obviously critical. His words echoed a sense of self-examination and social responsibility. Having a head's up on the extermination of their city, they became interested in all the steps needed to comply with Jonah's report.

Freewill had fueled their sins. The fear that they could be destroyed motivated a radical adjustment in their conduct. I believe these people discovered that the very thing they loved most was not worth dying for.

Think for a moment about those men, women, and children in Nineveh. With a renewed sense of self-worth, the realization of their spiritual needs had transcended beyond what vain and materialistic things they had previously coveted. Much like you and I, these individuals wanted peace in their homes and across their land. They wanted their children to play outside without the fear of pedophiles. The Ninevite community wanted legislature that represented them and their newly discovered faith in the Almighty God. Therefore the immigrant prophet, who came with critical words, became a beacon of hope for the survival of their nation. By the time that Jonah's memo reached the king, the people had already decided what type of life they desired.

By no means could the king have said no. The shift had taken place inside the social anatomy of the city. The spiritual infrastructure was turning over to make way for a reformation of faith and communal uplift. Before the king's nobles and other government officials had an opportunity to deceive, deny, and suppress the people's hopes, the fire of faith had already been set ablaze inside the capital's gates.

"This is not a trend," the king realized, "This is real and it is happening now."

The king made his royal decree from this experience and faith became law.

The Power To Deal

All of this started with one man. Jonah's renewed faith in God's plan gave him the determination to see the plan through. It had taken him only three days to turn a vile nation into a blessed, faithful one. We can no way foresee the results our faith can bring. By trusting in ourselves and standing on the promises of Christ, we can influence, even save, others from unfulfilled lives. Furthermore, when we use the power within us, we can reshape the reality of this world.

There will be occasions when we can clearly see the will of God moving throughout our circumstance. He often gives us a glimpse into His plan so that our focus does not shift. As a rule of thumbs all believers should know that we cannot expect God to honor any request without our full participation and complete submission. We must be willing to accept and seize every opportunity to employ our gift if we expect to see the promise materialize in our lives.

Faith is a guide that says all manmade limits are non-existent. Once we tap into this singular entity and its unlimited potential, this world will no longer become a challenge. No longer will you walk alone. Our minds will be at ease and our problems will no longer weigh as heavily in our spirit as they did before. This does not mean that you'll be free of worry. At times you may even entertain the speculative risks involved in a committed life under God's direction. Parked in the crux of your thoughts will often be a small specter of the unknown festering about in attempts to sway you from His will. However, the stronger your faith becomes, the more life will begin to surprise you. Your survey of the present and scope for the future will no longer seem as challenging.

In your masterful, faithful mind you will recognize your power to overcome all things. Moving forward, as issues arise, your perspective view of those things will be different. In the Lord you will discover that you have inherited something monumental – something that the fallen authorities of this world cannot take away.

MARK 5:34
FAITH IS ESSENTIAL
"And He said to her, "Daughter, your faith has made you well. Go in peace, and be healed of your affliction.""

Much of Jesus's ministry dealt with self-realization. The potential bubbling up within each of us only confirms that failure and success are limited by that which we are willing to do ourselves. Your gift, your purpose, and God's will are the components that will act as a catalyst for this generation's awakening. Begin today walking in faith and in the knowledge that you are what this world is missing.

The Backsliding Man

Jonah 4

*1 But it displeased Jonah exceedingly, and he became angry.
2 So he prayed to the LORD, and said, "Ah, LORD, was not
this what I said when I was still in my country? Therefore I fled
previously to Tarshish; for I know that You are a gracious and
merciful God, slow to anger and abundant in loving-kindness, One
who relents from doing harm.
3 Therefore now, O LORD, please take my life from me, for it is
better for me to die than to live!"
4 Then the LORD said, "Is it right for you to be angry?"
5 So Jonah went out of the city and sat on the east side of the city.
There he made himself a shelter and sat under it in the shade, till he
might see what would become of the city.
6 And the LORD God prepared a plant and made it come up over
Jonah, that it might be shade for his head to deliver him from his
misery. So Jonah was very grateful for the plant.
7 But as morning dawned the next day God prepared a worm, and it
so damaged the plant that it withered.
8 And it happened, when the sun arose, that God prepared a
vehement east wind; and the sun beat on Jonah's head, so that he
grew faint. Then he wished death for himself, and said, "It is better
for me to die than to live."
9 Then God said to Jonah, "Is it right for you to be angry about the
plant?" And he said, "It is right for me to be angry, even to death!"
10 But the LORD said, "You have had pity on the plant for which you
have not labored, nor made it grow, which came up in a night and
perished in a night.
11 And should I not pity Nineveh, that great city, in which are more
than one hundred and twenty thousand persons who cannot discern
between their right hand and their left—and much livestock?"*

Ok, maybe identifying Jonah as a "backslider" is a stretch. After all that he had been through as result of his insolence, Jonah reverted back to his emotions of displeasure toward God's Plan. He was successful in accomplishing the task in Nineveh but had immediately forgotten the underlining meaning of the mission. He also needed to be reminded that he was chosen specifically for the missionary trip.

We discovered how Jonah became the perfect candidate for this assignment. Salvation and mercy followed wherever Jonah went. The Prophet Jonah undoubtedly had the favor of God upon him. It was more than enough to qualify him as the proper deliverer of this message to the Ninevites.

It was important for God to create the testimony aside from Jonah's disobedience. Even in the depths of the sea, God was able to assess Jonah's personality flaws; actually, even before he dashed away from the task.

Who better to sympathize with us than someone that has dealt through similar situations?

Jonah's prayer for salvation made him the perfect liaison to speak to the people who had none. The citizens of Nineveh were undeserving of God's mercy. We all are undeserving. When commanding our gifts and abilities it's not up to us to decide who can receive them. Salvation has no registration period or application process. It belongs to us all, free of charge, and can only be issueed by the Lord. It certainly didn't belong solely to Jonah; although he attempted to withhold it from the Ninevites, as well as the sailors.

God had blessed the Hebrews, His chosen people. He had left them with a meticulous, yet necessary, system of law. God had also provided a homeland for the descendants of Abraham and now He was setting His focus on spreading His graciousness across the globe. God had searched the hearts of men and began to scout every nation to re-bridge the connection between Him and all of mankind. The veil had been immediately lifted from the eyes of the Ninevites and they had been redeemed. He was pleased.

Jonah, similarly, should have found pleasure in seeing the power of God's saving grace manifest throughout the city. Somehow, after all was said and done, he felt cheated. Jonah's selfishness had once again appeared. He had managed to take the Father's compassion for granted. He was livid about God's decision. He had already predicted the possibility of God executing His mercy, despite the threat, over Nineveh. Jonah already imagined the odds of God letting them off easy. He was absolutely right!

Our prophet displayed tolerance toward the Ninevites just long enough to fulfill God's command. In hindside, he had hoped that God would follow through with destroying the city. Because the Father withheld destruction, it seems as though there was still a great deal of resentment housed in Jonah's heart.

The prophet's timely message of salvation was prolific and their actions immediately reflected their acceptance of it. However, as he hiked up the nearest hillside to look back at the city, a cloud of bitterness hung over him. He had succumbed to anger once more.

Anger Management

As he attempted to avoid the heat of the Sun, he seemed to still have the pressure of the mission upon him. His temperament became volatile. Jonah's anger had festered into self-indulged tension that was only heightened by the punishing heat of the Sun. Jonah took shade under a tree with low hanging fruit. He awaited the destruction of the city but God had relented His great wrath upon the people. Jonah gave it another day just in case God decided otherwise. The day drew slowly to a close and evening came. Jonah's fury grew even more.

God allowed a gourd, or large hanging fruit, to grow on a nearby branch to give Jonah a moment to relax his nerve. God was basically telling Jonah to "take a chill pill" instead of being distraught about the nearly demolished city of Nineveh.

Jonah sat himself comfortably under the tree so that the branch and fruit hid him from the intense heat.

Jonah wasn't good at reading between the lines. He figured that the people could use a little forgiveness and mercy, but in his twisted mind, they also deserved to die. Jonah had no mercy for the Ninevites. After all he had been through he still wished death on his enemies.

It's unique that God held His hand against the city, but what's more incredible than that is the power of a second chance at life. The prophet neglected to see the nature of the Creator in the universal scheme of things. His enemies were no longer a threat to him or the nation of Israel. They were no longer war torn. They all shared a common bond – complete faith and submission to the Everlasting God of Creation.

In addition to Jonah's bitter attitude, he had also ignored the fact that had these people died their blood would have been on his hands. Similar would have been the case regarding the seafarers aboard the Tarshish-bound ship. By taking away the gourd and setting the sunlight on Jonah's brow, God reminded Jonah that only He had the authority to give and take life.

Jonah was in an awesome position to foresee the spiritual shift that God was setting up for future generations. The Creator demonstrated His control over Death. This control would eventually reverberate across the world. God, however, was not ready to show this to everyone. The time would come soon. Death would be defeated, controlled, and enslaved before all men when He proclaimed the mortal birth and arrival of His Son, Jesus.

The Lesson Learned

God has full authority to do whatever he wills; His thoughts and plans are beyond our understanding. We can only accept His ultimatums and modify our lives likewise. To not comply with his commandments will bring about the hardships we frequently encounter. No man can measure the footprint of God or know the secrets of His mind. He does not have to disclose the reasons why He has sent us toward a destined place. All He asks is that we submit and move.

God is required to set provisions to allow the blueprints of His word to come to fruition – that is where you and I come in. The *Lord's Prayer* states, "Thou will be done on Earth as it is in Heaven." This is not a statement we should take likely. If we believe that angels carry out His plans in the heavenly realm, who do you think must do the work here on Earth? That's right – Us!

Jonah learned a valuable lesson, but we have made this mistake as well. God may send you somewhere to do something that doesn't make sense. You may find yourself working with a horrible employer or with an organization whose values don't align with your own. Trust and believe that our steps are ordered. Therefore, we must keep our feet to the ground and reflect on God purpose. Be sure to pray concerning His plan for you. Prayer can help you proceed pass the storms that beat against your confidence and freedom.

Trust God in every detail of your life. Do not let the uncertainty of this life clog your spiritual growth. Nor should you allow spontaneous outcomes to scatter your passion away from God's plan in your life.

....

ROMANS 8:28
FROM TRAGEDY TO TRIUMPH
"And we know that all things work together for good to those who love God, to those who are the called according to His purpose."
....

The Man and His Message

Luke 11:29-32

29 As the crowds were increasing, He began to say, "This generation is a wicked generation; it seeks for a sign, and yet no sign will be given to it but the sign of Jonah.

30 For just as Jonah became a sign to the Ninevites, so will the Son of Man be to this generation.

31 The Queen of the South will rise up with the men of this generation at the judgment and condemn them, because she came from the ends of the earth to hear the wisdom of Solomon; and behold, something greater than Solomon is here.

32 The men of Nineveh will stand up with this generation at the judgment and condemn it, because they repented at the preaching of Jonah; and behold, something greater than Jonah is here.

Now that you've read the entire book inspired by the life of the Prophet Jonah, you are well on your way to achieve your highest potential and should have a renewed vision of your life. A few of you will have the burden of rediscovering who you are. There will be those who will find an interest in the story as I had and be left with one final question. For me, after being extensively engaged in *The Book of Jonah* for several months, there remained a lingering thought.

Since I had dissected the moral lessons from the prophet's brief narrative, I could not help but to wonder why the author, assumingly Jonah, would only write of these events. With a lifetime full of trials and lessons learned, was this the only thing he found interesting to be remembered by? Why would Jonah expose his faults to us?

As I reflected on my investigative queries, I was brought back to the very instance that inspired me to begin this study. After much prayer and meditation, it was revealed to me. I received a vision of myself - the future me. While in meditation, Jonah's intentions spoke through, loudly and clearly.

The Bad Is Meant For Good, For Others

Being the esteemed spiritual figure of his day, Prophet Jonah debated what he'd write and how he would portray himself. He'd have nothing to gain by painting a glamorous image of himself to the hundreds of generations of God-fearing men and women that would proceed after. Thankfully he was honest – brief – but honest nonetheless.

To Jonah, there was no benefit in sharing all of the virtuous instances in his ministry. The Honorable Prophet understood that if he must tell his story it must impact us on the personal level. Hence, it would serve best to describe the moments where the condition of his manhood and spiritual identity were being trialed. He dedicated his last will and testament to the pressure test he endured. His wish was for us to learn something new about ourselves and to encourage us through the issues of life. It is in our doubts, our tests, our storms, and in darkness when we should desperately begin to seek God for courage. These are the moments that define us and shape our tomorrow.

There would be no prize in Jonah displaying himself as the hero. The Apostle Paul certainly agrees. In his second letter to the church in Corinth, Apostle Paul says, "...I will not boast about myself, except about my weaknesses." (2 Corinthian 12:5 NIV)

Having a story that is relatable, personable, and considerably relevant to each unique individual speaks volumes. It compels us all to identify not only with the character of the story, but with every human heart on the planet.

As the Christian movement began to witness expansion, having sanctified leadership gave early Christians an available example to follow. Even the great apostles understood that spotlighting the best in him would have proven to be ineffective in establishing a relationship with the people. From the various churches across the Aegean Islands to mainland Greece, these apostles spoke from their own personal experiences in Christ to help radically transform their community and culture.

The Personal Connection

After all the words were scribed and the ink had dried, Jonah realized that it wasn't about him. He allowed us to gain a glimpse into his disruptive, indecisive, and obscure ministry to show that he was a man. No man is perfect. No ministry is perfect. We are always in a phase of development. It's impossible for any of us to claim that we have it all figured out. Shamefully, we have not been virtuous to our own reflection. We have failed in our relationships. We often come up short on our commitments.

Thankfully this does not mean you can't be used by God. Your inconsistent, compulsive behavior does not disqualify you of the potential sowed within you by grace. Jonah finally understood that he was no different than we are. Regardless of what state of spiritual hell you are in, it's not too late. You're in the perfect position to be utilized. If you've acknowledged your own personal faults, now is the time for you to listen to the voice of God. The prophet listened the second time, but consider what he had to endure.

At some point we must all give an account for our sins. We must face our shame and confront God in all humility. The best part is that you don't have to be afraid to do this because he already knows. As a child of the Omniscient Creator, it is your right to be forgiven and have a fresh start. Jonah accepted death over redemption. I'm positive that as he looked back over his decisions he must have felt like an idiot.

He put himself through so much. Jonah fled out of fear and the only thing that came from it was more fear. That's no way for anyone to live. Waking up each day to another uncomfortable situation or opening our eyes to a brand new uncertainty – that's not the life God has intended for us.

By recording the mistakes he made in his ministry, Jonah speaks to the hearts of men to encourage us to evaluate ourselves during each step of our faith walk. We are all blessed with an untapped source of potential. As a matter of fact, we are all connected to one true source – our heavenly Father. We are called to serve one another. Jonah's duty was to introduce the path of salvation to those who had not known it before. The Prophet Jonah's view shifted as God continued to shape his heart.

Final Thoughts

Throughout Heaven's Headache we discover that this mission

was also a "beta test" for God's redemptive love to stretch across each nation, to every soul on Earth. The seed of purpose in Jonah seemed to be no more than a prophetic speech to the Ninevites. Jonah's mission to Nineveh was an opportunity for faith to flourish in this world. Ultimately, that seed became one of the first roots in the ground toward beginning the establishment of the Kingdom of God.

The people of that great city saw faith as a new invention, a new deal. Their acceptance of this intangible gift of the spirit is powerful in the sense that they received it as soon as it was offered. This message ordained by the God was remarkably taken seriously by roughly 100 thousand citizens.

Imagine if you were sick and received a prescription called *Faith*. After its benefits and side effects are thoroughly explained, would you try it, or would you be a skeptic? Would you read the label and comb through reviews online before taking it? Well, many of the Israelites had flat out refused it. However, this was a limited-time opportunity for the people of Nineveh. Jonah had arrived and had no intentions on coming back. Considering the severity of his speech he realized this had to be his best presentation ever. If he hadn't made the commit to minister to the people, he would have disrupted the plan to introduce faith as a mode of communion with God for generations to come.

Jonah realized that we would become the fruits of his success in the city of Nineveh. Properly earning his title, the Prophet Jonah assisted in a grassroots crusade for the Kingdom to be established here on Earth. What would transpire from this chapter in history would lead to an even more monumental event – the birth of Jesus of Nazareth.

This new path in faith was vital and lead to a full-blown spiritual movement centuries later. This movement over time grew into a revolution that not only altered the religious institution, but also the geographical landscape, culture, as well as traditions across the globe. Jesus spoke frequently of the essentiality of a faithful life so much that it was later stated by the Apostle Paul that "it is impossible to please God" without it. Faith is necessary right now.

. . . .

PSALMS 40:4
ALLEGIANCE TO GOD
"How blessed is the man who has made the LORD his trust, And has not turned to the proud, nor to those who lapse into falsehood."

. . . .

The corporatizing of our bodies by the pillars of society has tossed many people's souls into a mindlessness abyss. Various bureaucracies have put systems in place to condition us away from the faithful lives we are supposed to experience daily. Your citizenship in the Kingdom of God, through Christ Jesus, is of more value than any partisan affiliation, allegiance, concept, or notion that we can promote or buy into. Faith was created for us and must be carried on by us. We are entitled to God's everlasting love and mercy. Don't wait to stake your claim.

The purpose within you is for all in the world to enjoy. You are as much a part of me as I am a part of you – we are the church, Christ's assemblage.

Jonah understood that he could not hide his sins from us. His message is our message. His life is our life. With this incredible knowledge, you can begin to ignite your gift and fuel it with the limitless potential that is within you. All that is and shall be from this day forward is set in motion by God's operative love. The power to move forward into greatness in life is in your possession. Activate it today.

Seek God first and he will direct your path.

References

New King James Version® Copyright 1982 by Thomas Nelson, Inc.

Scriptures were referenced from The Bible Gateway www.biblegateway.com Bible Gateway 10 East 53rd Street New York, NY 10022 operated by The Zondervan Corporation, L.L.C.

THE PROPHETS. Copyright © 1962 by Abraham J. Heschel. HarperCollins Publishers Inc., 10 East 53rd Street, New York, NY 10022. ISBN 978-0-06-093699-0

Music Industry Statistics courtesy of The Nielsen Company & Billboard's 2011 Music Industry Report http://www.businesswire.com/news/home/20120105005547/en/Nielsen-Company-Billboard%E2%80%99s-2011-Music-Industry-Report

Vailhé, S. (1912). Tarsus. In The Catholic Encyclopedia. New York: Robert Appleton Company. Retrieved October 2, 2013 from New Advent: http://www. newadvent.org/cathen/14461b.htm

International World History Project: World History From The Pre-Sumerian Period To The Present. History-World.org Copyright © 1995 – 2006 [World History Project, USA] http://history-world.org/nineveh.htm. http://history-world.org/assyria_part_sixteen.htm.

Online Parallel Bible © 2004-2013 by Biblos.com. http://bibleatlas.org/tarshish.htm

History Of The Cross: The pagan origin and idolatrous adoption and worship of the image © 1871 by Henry Dana Ward, M.A.. London | (Philadelphia, Claxton, Remsen, & Heffelfinger) *source: original from Princeton University

Todd Bolen, "The Pool of Siloam Revealed," BiblePlaces.com. http://www. bibleplaces.com/joppa.htm.

Blank, Wayne © Daily Bible Study http://www.keyway.ca/htm2002/jonah.htm

Encyclopædia Britannica © 1994-2013 by Encyclopædia Britannica, Inc. www.britannica.com/EBchecked/topic/39661/Astarte

Appreciation to Simon Sinek for his book *Start With Why*, Copyright © 2009. Penguin Group (USA), New York, New York 10014. All rights reserved.

Robert H. Schuller *Tough Times Never Last but Tough People Do* (1983), Thomas Nelson: ISBN 978-0-8407-5287-1

Credits & Acknowledgements

All credit due to the Most High God.

Much love and extreme gratitude to my wife and daughter.

Special thanks to my parents, Muriel and Randolph Sr., as well as to my sibling's and their families.

Appreciation extended to the entire Knighten and King families and to my hometown, the city of Baker, Louisiana.

CPSIA information can be obtained
at www.ICGtesting.com
Printed in the USA
FSHW011952021218
54195FS

9 780991 141210